EXPLORE
my world

Sea Otters

Jill Esbaum

NATIONAL
GEOGRAPHIC
KiDS

WASHINGTON, D.C.

Hello, sea otters!

These furry floaters rock and roll with the never-ending waves. *Splish, splash, sploosh!*

A group of sea otters is called a raft.

Playful sea otters spin and twirl and romp together.

They chase. They dive.
They pop up. Surprise!

One slips under, swimming down, down, down, to search the ocean floor for abalone and clams.

An abalone is a type of big sea snail.

clamshell

To open a stubborn shell,
the otter puts a rock on
her chest. She whacks
the shell against it until ...

Ta-da!

Each day, sea otters spend several hours grooming themselves. A clean coat is important!

Rub-a-dub-scrub!

After her meal, the sea otter washes her face and neck.

Using her teeth and claws, she combs her coat until every inch is smooth and shiny.

Snuggle.

A pup rides his mother's chest, cuddling close, comfy cozy.

The mother otter nurses her baby, then grooms and fluffs his thick fur.

baby sea otter fur

The pup was born in the water, but he cannot swim. Not yet.

Still, he's safe.
The air trapped inside
his fluffy, puffy coat
keeps him afloat.

A pup's air-filled fluff makes going underwater impossible, even if it wanted to.

15

kelp

Before the mother otter dives for food, she wraps her pup in kelp to keep him from drifting away.

When she disappears, the pup worries and whines—*eek, eek, eek.*

He can only wait, bobbing like a fuzzy cork.

Near the seafloor, the mother weaves through swaying stalks of kelp, on the lookout for ... an urchin!

sea urchin

Back on the surface, she crunches it with her sharp teeth. Yum!

A few months later, a sleek fur coat has replaced the pup's fluff.

He's learned to swim
and hunt, to dive and play,
and to groom himself.

Ride on, sea otter!

Rock and roll with the never-ending waves. *Splish, splash, sploosh.*

Look at me: I'm waterproof!

A sea otter's thick fur grows in two layers. The underfur, next to its skin, is soft and fluffy. Over that are long guard hairs that act like a raincoat. As long as an otter's fur is clean, water has a hard time getting through!

Is your hair long or short?

Do you fluff your hair after it's washed?

After grooming, a sea otter rolls in the water, using its paws to fluff air back into its coat.

Your head holds about 100,000 hairs. A sea otter's coat has as many as a million hairs in every square inch!

25

Perfect Paradise

The cold waters of the Pacific Ocean's northern coastlines make perfect homes for sea otters. Here's why:

Do you live near water?

Can you float on your back like a sea otter?

Would you rather swim in cold water or warm water?

26

1 **They're shallow.** It's only a short dive to the seafloor, where sea otters find their food.

2 **Land is only a short swim away.** Even though they spend most of their lives in the water, some sea otters like to come onto the beach to rest or sleep.

3 **Kelp forests grow here.** Sea otters wrap themselves in kelp so they won't float away while sleeping. Kelp forests are another place to find food, too.

kelp

Seafood Snack Bar

clams

Have you tasted crabs or clams?

crab

Sea otters like to eat the meat inside abalone, crabs, clams, mussels, and snails. They also like soft creatures such as squid and octopus.

octopus

Sea otters even help keep kelp forests healthy. How? By eating the sea urchins that eat and destroy the bottom of kelp stalks.

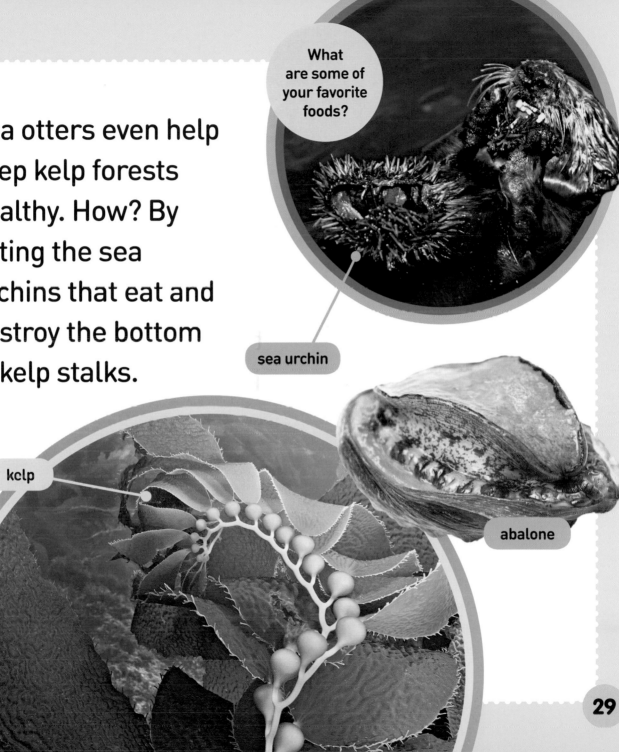

What are some of your favorite foods?

sea urchin

kclp

abalone

29

Home of the Sea Otter

Sea otters live in parts of the North Pacific Ocean.

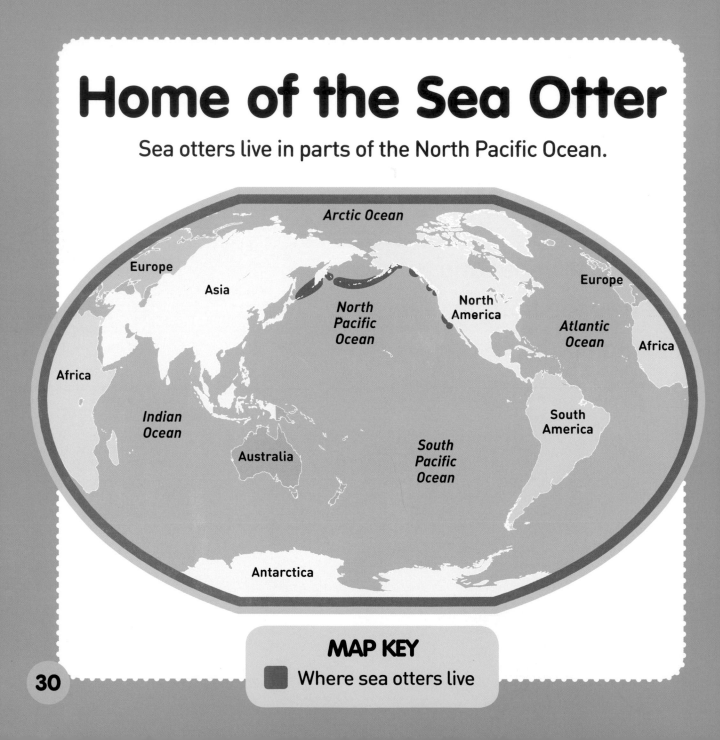

Arctic Ocean

Europe

Asia

North Pacific Ocean

North America

Europe

Atlantic Ocean

Africa

Africa

Indian Ocean

South America

Australia

South Pacific Ocean

Antarctica

MAP KEY

Where sea otters live

Sea Otter Search

With your finger, help the baby sea otter find its mother. Say the names of the other things the baby otter sees along the way.

For Frederick and Eli—JE

Published by National Geographic Partners, LLC. All rights reserved. Reproduction of the whole or any part of the contents without written permission from the publisher is prohibited.

Since 1888, the National Geographic Society has funded more than 12,000 research, exploration, and preservation projects around the world. The Society receives funds from National Geographic Partners, LLC, funded in part by your purchase. A portion of the proceeds from this book supports this vital work. To learn more, visit natgeo.com/info.

NATIONAL GEOGRAPHIC and Yellow Border Design are trademarks of the National Geographic Society, used under license.

Library of Congress Cataloging-in-Publication Data

Names: Esbaum, Jill, author.
Title: Sea otters / Jill Esbaum.
Other titles: Explore my world.
Description: Edition 1. | Washington, DC : National Geographic, [2017] | Series: Explore my world | Audience: Ages 3-7. | Audience: K to grade 3.
Identifiers: LCCN 2016050205 (print) | LCCN 2016053550 (ebook) | ISBN 9781426328251 (pbk. : alk. paper) | ISBN 9781426328268 (hardcover : alk. paper) | ISBN 9781426328275 (e-book)
Subjects: LCSH: Sea otter--Juvenile literature.
Classification: LCC QL737.C25 E81995 2017 (print) | LCC QL737.C25 (ebook) | DDC 599.769/5--dc23
LC record available at https://lccn.loc.gov/2016050205

The publisher gratefully acknowledges Kim Steinhardt, board member, Long Marine Lab's Seymour Discovery Center at the University of California, Santa Cruz, for his expert review of this book.

Art director and designer: Amanda Larsen

Printed in Hong Kong
17/THK/1

ILLUSTRATIONS CREDITS
Front cover, Michael Quinton/Minden Pictures; Back cover (LO), Design Pics Inc/National Geographic Creative; 1 (CTR), Milo Burcham/Getty Images; 2–3 (CTR), Donald M. Jones/Minden Pictures; 4–5 (CTR), Mint Images/Frans Lanting/Getty Images; 6 (UP), Jane Smith/SeaPics.com; 6 (LO), Jody Overstreet; 7 (CTR), Cameron Rutt/Getty Images; 8 (CTR), Bates Littlehales/Getty Images; 9 (UP LE), Tamara Kulikova/Shutterstock; 9 (UP RT), Kim Steinhardt; 9 (LO), Phillip Colla/SeaPics.com; 10–11, Tom & Pat Leeson; 12 (CTR), Design Pics Inc/National Geographic Creative; 13 (UP), Chase Dekker Wild-Life Images/Getty Images; 13 (LO), Monterey Bay Aquarium; 14–15 Donald M. Jones/Minden Pictures; 16–17 (LE), Doc White/SeaPics.com; 18 (UP), Francois Gohier/Alamy Stock Photo; 18 (LO), photossee/Shutterstock; 19 (CTR), Norbert Wu/Minden Pictures; 20 (CTR), Donald M. Jones/Minden Pictures; 21, Tom & Pat Leeson; 22–23 (CTR), KenCanning/Getty Images; 24 (LO), Chase Dekker Wild-Life Images/Getty Images; 25 (CTR), Harry Walker; 26 (UP), Juanmonino/Getty Images; 26 (LO), Design Pics Inc/National Geographic Creative; 26 (LO LE), Mark Newman/Getty Images; 27 (UP), hkomala/Shutterstock; 27 (CTR), Jurgen and Christine Sohns/Minden Pictures; 27 (LO), divindk/Getty Images; 28 (UP), tetxu/Shutterstock; 28 (LE), Volodymyr Krasyuk/Shutterstock; 28 (LO RT), Rich Reid/Getty Images; 29 (UP RT), Frans Lanting/National Geographic Creative; 29 (CTR RT), Jiang Hongyan/Shutterstock; 29 (LO), NatalieJean/Shutterstock; 31 (UP RT), Jim Capwell; 31, Jiang Zhongyan/Shutterstock; 31 (CTR RT), Tamara Kulikova/Shutterstock; 31 (UP LE), photossee/Shutterstock; 31 (LO), Donald M. Jones/Minden Pictures; 32 (LO), Patrick Endres/Design Pics/Getty Images